Airlift fias...

Rwandans ...home as aid ...sses targets

CSA PAY BUNGL... LEFT ME BRO...

EXCLUSIVE By ROGER TODD

A DIVORCED father has wrongly had £634 a month docked from his pay by the Child Support Agency.

The outrageous bungle forced crane driver ... Sullivan to:

PUT his £40,000 house up for sale.

SELL his Ford Escort ... and

HAVE his phone cut off.

Desperate 36-year-old ... is now off work ... from a stomach ... stress. ... the CSA ... puter for ...

agency fixed Roy's maintenance deductions at £1,004 a month.

Then it found he was being charged not only for his two daughters – but for a child who isn't his.

The agency apologised and reduced the deduction order attached to his earnings.

But Roy, from Cardiff, still hasn't had a refund. He said: "I earn £300 a week but after deductions I didn't have enough left to pay my £300 mortgage.

"I've had the 'For Sale' sign up for several weeks ...rests of justice over... the PIIC does no... my view."

"My bank manager can't see any option as I haven't any money left to live on.

"I appealed against the CSA assessment ... summer but they ... no notice. The... forced my emp... hand it all over... "I can't bel... dictatorial ... agency behav...

Appa...

Labour ... Jones, w... Roy's ... appalli... "Th... bank... big... m... le...

© Aladdin Books Ltd 1995

Designed and produced by
Aladdin Books Ltd
28 Percy Street
London W1P 0LD

First published in Great Britain in 1995 by
Watts Books
96 Leonard Street
London EC2A 4RH

Editor: Katie Roden
Designer: Gary Edgar-Hyde
Illustrator: David Burroughs
Picture research: Brooks Krikler Research

Terry Brown (author) is an independent consultant, trainer and writer in health education.
Adrian King (co-author and consultant) has worked as a teacher and a youth and community worker. He is currently a health education coordinator for a local education authority.

Printed in Belgium

All rights reserved

A CIP catalogue record for this book is available from the British Library

ISBN: 0 7496 2177 X

TOPICS... HOT TOPICS... HOT TOPICS... HOT

Special Edition   1

DRUGS

An Issue for Everyone

Terry Brown and Adrian King

Some people think that it should be legal to use the drug cannabis.

A WATTS BOOK
LONDON • SYDNEY • LONDON • SYDNEY • LONDON • SYDNEY • LONDON • SYDNEY

TOPICS... HOT TOPICS... HOT TOPICS... HOT

Introduction: A Drug-Using Society 2

An Everyday Issue

MODERN WESTERN society is a drug-using society. Legal and illegal drugs are taken for various reasons, but their availability and dangerous use are causing great concern and debate in many countries.

INSIDE

Introduction	2-3

IN THE NEWS

The Spread of Drug Use	4-5
An International Concern	6-7
Drugs and the Media	8-9

WHAT IS A DRUG?

The Facts about Drug Use	10-11
The History of Drug Use	12-13
The Risks to Health	14-15
Laws and Restrictions	16-17
Tracking the Cargoes	18-19
Where to Turn	20-21
Conflicts of Opinion	22-23

LATEST NEWS

Drugs in the Public Eye	24-25
A Growing Occurrence?	26-27
A New Approach	28-29
What Can We Do?	30
Glossary	31
Index	32

Legal drugs are familiar to us all. If people go to the doctor, they are given drugs as medicine. Tea, coffee and cola contain the drug caffeine. In most countries it is legal to drink alcohol and to smoke tobacco, which contains the drug nicotine. Some legal substances, such as glue, may be misused, while anabolic steroids are legal to use but illegal to sell and are misused to improve sporting ability.

The use of illegal drugs, such as cannabis, cocaine, crack, LSD and Ecstasy, is common. This can lead users into danger, and may cause illness and even death. For years, police forces and customs all over the world have waged a 'war' on drugs, yet drug use continues to spread. Should governments now consider new ways of tackling the situation? Is there a good case for reviewing the legal status of some drugs?

In the Netherlands, it is legal to buy cannabis in some cafés.

TOPICS... HOT TOPICS... HOT TOPICS... HOT

Introduction: A Drug-Using Society

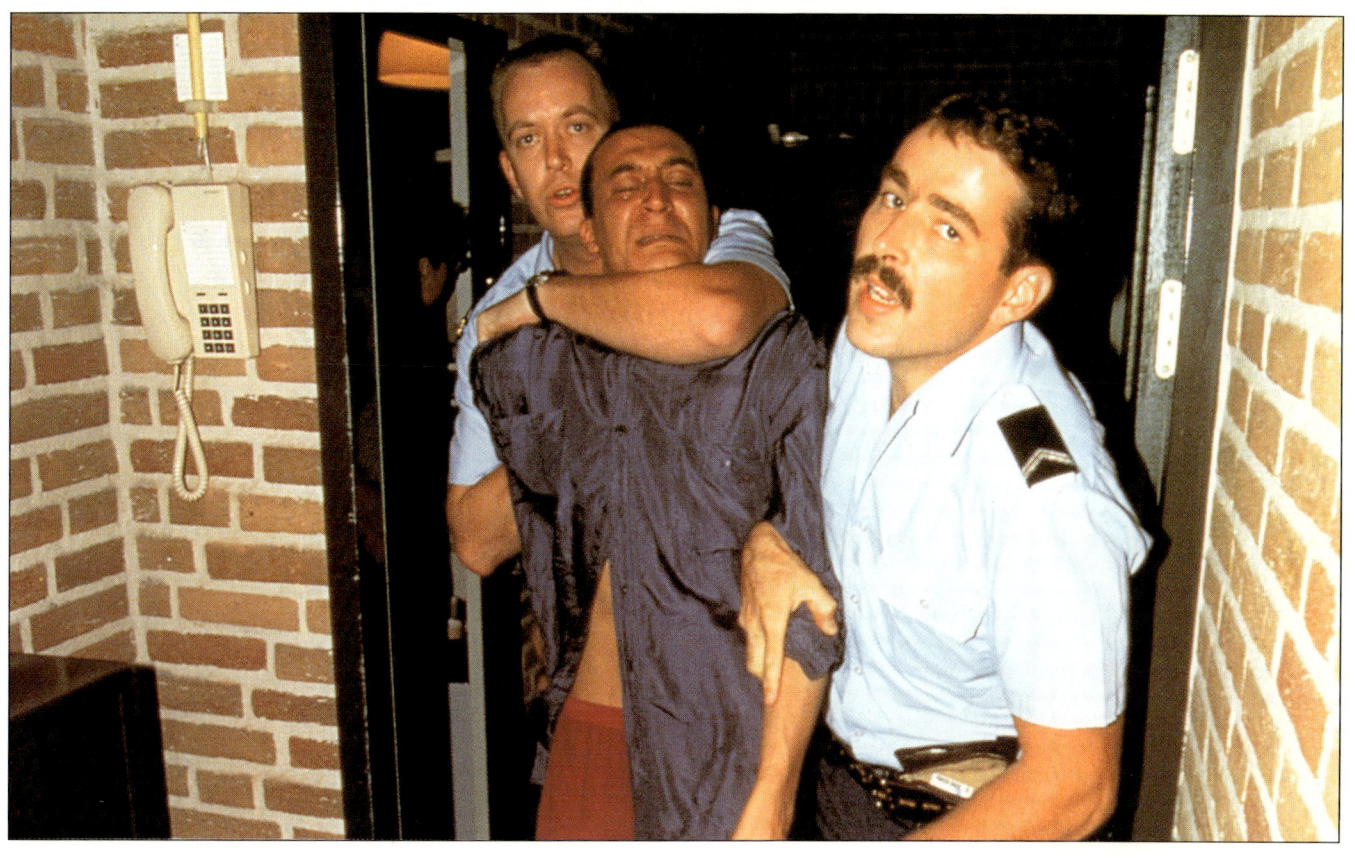

Arresting a drug dealer. Many people believe that the 'war' on drugs is not working.

Is There a *'Right'* Approach?

THE LEGAL status of drugs varies from country to country. Similarly, the ways in which different countries treat drug smugglers, dealers and users can also vary greatly, from harsh punishments to treatment and counselling.

Many people are now starting to doubt whether waging 'war' on the illegal drugs trade is the only method of dealing with the problem. They say that balanced advice and education are better ways of treating the subject. They will lessen the demand for drugs and so reduce the power of the suppliers and pushers.

Others claim that education will not stop people trying illegal drugs, or discourage people from selling them. They use the example of cigarette smoking: despite frequent campaigns about the dangers of tobacco, many young people experiment with cigarettes, and the age at which they do so is getting lower.

Today there is much debate about the legal status of some drugs, and about the way in which drug offenders should be treated by the law if caught. Should all offenders receive harsh punishments, or should the traffickers, who supply the drugs, be treated differently to the people who use them (and who might need help)?

TOPICS... HOT TOPICS... HOT TOPICS... HOT

In the News: The Spread of Drug Use   4

Children younger than ten may be involved in drug misuse.

Drugs a Danger to Young Pupils

STUDIES SHOW that most primary schools have pupils who are aware of or involved in drug use.

The age of starting to smoke tobacco and drink alcohol is getting lower and lower, and a few primary school pupils smoke and drink regularly. Children as young as six may be sniffing solvents, while younger pupils are often aware that older children are selling or using drugs.

Many children learn about drugs before they start school, from television programmes and films for example. Some may get involved with drugs at a very young age. This has led to calls for widespread drugs education classes, and for stricter controls over television programmes for young people.

Why Do We Do It?

People give various reasons for taking illegal drugs, such as:
to relieve pain;
to rebel against authority;
out of curiosity;
to escape from reality;
for pleasure;
to be sociable;
because the drugs are offered;
to fit in with a crowd;

People have many reasons for taking drugs.

to improve performance;
to relax;
to take a risk;
to impress;
pressure from other people;
to look older or 'cool';
to celebrate.
These reasons are commonly given for the use, and misuse, of legal drugs, in particular alcohol and tobacco.

TOPICS... HOT TOPICS... HOT TOPICS... HOT

In the News: The Spread of Drug Use 5

Hidden Risks Come to Light

Street Drugs Mixed with Deadly Impurities

YOU DON'T KNOW what you're getting when you buy illegal drugs. Recently, drugs sold in clubs have been found to contain lethal substances.

Ecstasy tablets, used at raves and clubs, might in fact be a mixture of amphetamine and LSD. Stock cubes may be sold as 'cannabis', while pure heroin may be combined with dangerous substances like fish-tank cleaner or painkillers. All sorts of pills may be sold as recreational drugs. These impurities can be dangerous to users, as they are hard to spot.

When you are given medicine by a doctor, the drugs have been tested for safety and you will be given instructions about how much to take. The quality and strength of alcohol and tobacco are also checked regularly. This is not true of drugs bought illegally, and users can be in great danger.

Ecstasy tablets sold at raves may, in fact, be made from other dangerous substances.

TOPICS... HOT TOPICS... HOT TOPICS... HOT

In the News: An International Concern 6

A Complicated Network which is Still Expanding

TOBACCO, ALCOHOL, medicines and illegal drugs all start with raw materials. These are processed and marketed, then sold through worldwide sales networks. These networks, for legal and illegal drugs, have become big business.

In the production of legal drugs, such as caffeine or medicines, each stage is inspected by the right authorities, and quality controls are applied. The people involved in the process are protected by workplace rules and insurance, have a regular income, and pay taxes to their governments.

The production and sale of illegal drugs make lots of money for a few people. Most of the workers involved have no legal protection and are in constant danger of being caught. They only make money if they sell the drug, which can often be difficult and very dangerous.

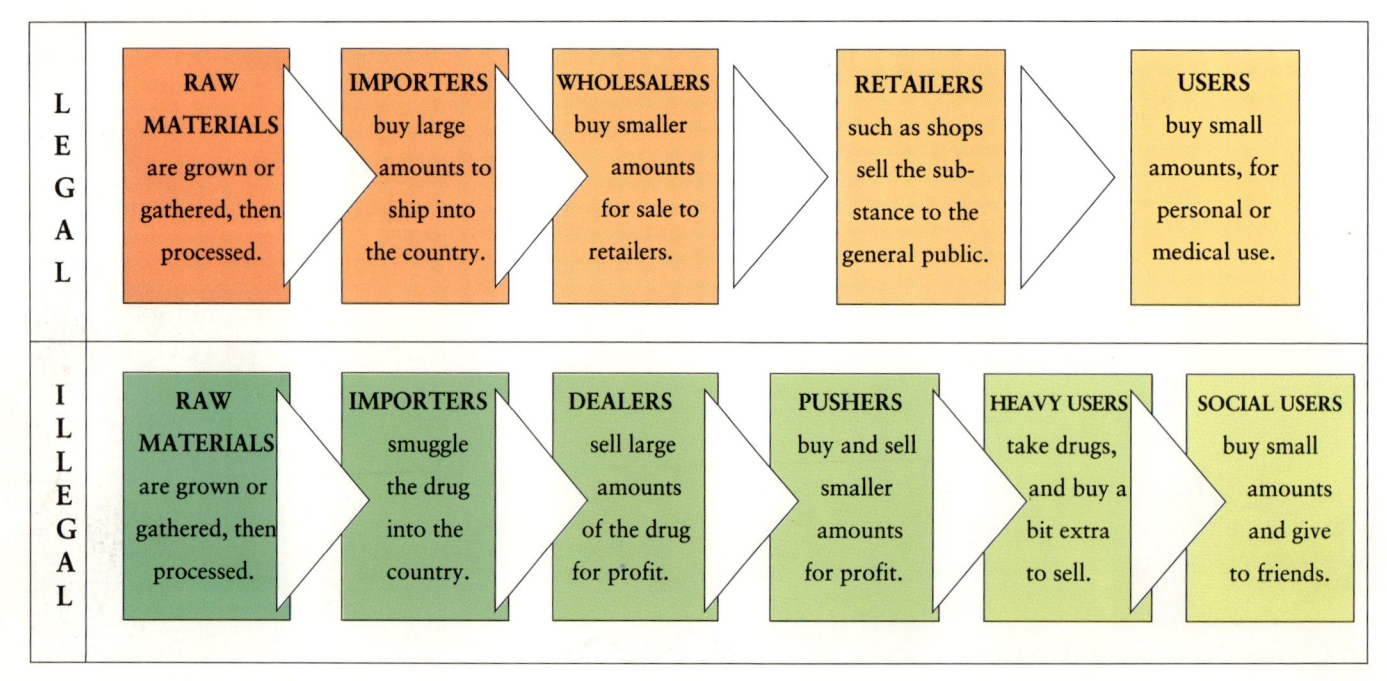

A field of opium poppies.

LEGAL

| RAW MATERIALS are grown or gathered, then processed. | IMPORTERS buy large amounts to ship into the country. | WHOLESALERS buy smaller amounts for sale to retailers. | RETAILERS such as shops sell the substance to the general public. | USERS buy small amounts, for personal or medical use. |

ILLEGAL

| RAW MATERIALS are grown or gathered, then processed. | IMPORTERS smuggle the drug into the country. | DEALERS sell large amounts of the drug for profit. | PUSHERS buy and sell smaller amounts for profit. | HEAVY USERS take drugs, and buy a bit extra to sell. | SOCIAL USERS buy small amounts and give to friends. |

The distribution networks of legal and illegal drugs.

TOPICS... HOT TOPICS... HOT TOPICS... HOT

In the News: An International Concern

Once involved in the drugs world, it can be very hard to escape.

A Dangerous Relationship

THE EVERYDAY buyers of illegal drugs are at the end of a long line of activity, which begins with top-level criminals and huge amounts of money.

Throughout the drugs trade, the sellers have power over the buyers. The sellers demand high payments for their drugs, which can lead users into debt. Violence and threats are common at the highest levels, and there are many stories of gang warfare and 'contract killings'.

If users need a regular supply of a drug, it can become very hard for them to pay off these debts, and a few may turn to crimes such as stealing. It is often difficult for a person in this situation to seek support and protection from others, or to find legal help.

The Small-Time Drugs Industry

All over the world, illegal drugs are now being produced on a small scale in people's homes. This makes them very difficult for the police to track down. Some synthetic drugs, such as amphetamines, can be made with simple equipment and chemicals which can be easily obtained. Cannabis plants are cultivated under specially designed growing lights, both for personal use and to sell. The increase in home-grown cannabis has led many people to argue for the legalisation of the drug. They claim that home-growing reduces the risk of drug users getting into debt and so being in danger from drug dealers and crime.

Cannabis can be home-grown.

TOPICS... HOT TOPICS... HOT TOPICS... HOT

In the News: Drugs and the Media

The Advertising Debate

ADVERTISING IS used both to sell legal drugs and to stop the use of illegal ones. This often presents very confusing messages, and many people are now campaigning for new advertising laws.

Legal drugs such as tobacco and alcohol are advertised on hoardings, in cinemas and on television all over the world. Many people think that such advertising should be banned, so that it cannot tempt young people to try the products. The advertisers claim that it only persuades smokers and drinkers to change the brands they use, and does not encourage people to start smoking or drinking. It is difficult to find figures to prove either of these arguments. Large tobacco companies give much-needed money to some countries, so their governments do not want to ban cigarette advertising.

Some people are trying to ban the advertising of legal drugs.

Familiar Images

We are constantly surrounded by indirect advertising, or advertising which we do not always notice. These forms of advertising can work very well, because people do not realise they are being sold a product by the manufacturers. Tobacco and alcohol companies sponsor popular sporting events such as motor racing, football championships and snooker tournaments. 'Product placement' is used in television programmes and films. How often have you seen the names of products clearly displayed during a movie? You may not realise it, but this is also a form of paid advertising.

Conflicting messages.

TOPICS... HOT TOPICS... HOT TOPICS... HOT

In the News: Drugs and the Media

Newspapers and magazines often print dramatic drugs stories to attract readers.

Drugs Stories a Weapon in the Newspaper Wars

NEWSPAPERS EXIST to inform, to entertain, and to increase their readership. They constantly compete with each other to attract the most readers. These factors can affect the way in which the drugs issue is treated.

Newspapers and television programmes (the media) can seem to take a very strict, anti-drugs attitude. As part of this they present shocking stories, to put people off using drugs and to prove to their readers or viewers that the media are 'respectable'. Many people learn about drugs and drug use from the TV and newspapers, yet the media do not always give a balanced picture. Although many newspapers are responsible and try to report the truth about the drugs situation, the dramatic stories described by others are not necessarily the experience of all people who take drugs. Almost all illegal drugs were first used as medicines, and still have some positive medical effects if used correctly. Some media organisations try to show all the facts about drugs, so that their readers can form their own considered opinions, but it is important that they all do this.

What is a Drug? 10

The Facts about Drug Use

Depressants slow the nervous system and relax the body. Alcohol (above) is the most common, but other legal depressants are abused for these effects. These include barbiturates (sleeping pills), tranquillisers and solvents (glue and gases, below).

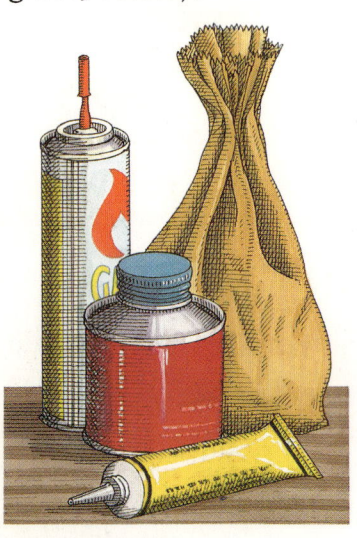

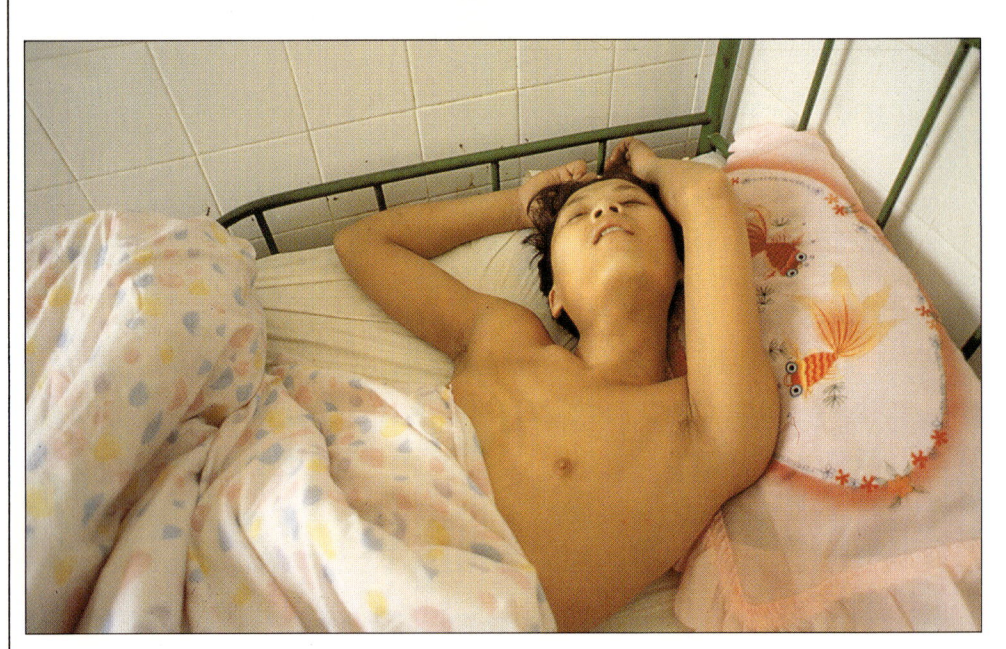

When users stop taking drugs, they may get withdrawal symptoms.

THE WORD 'DRUG' means any substance (except food) which affects the mind or the body. The effect depends on the type of drug, the amount taken, when and how it is used, and the person who takes it.

There are four levels of drug use. Abstinence means not taking any drugs or any particular drug. Experimentation means trying a drug for the first time. It could be a doctor prescribing medicine, or a young person sniffing glue. If a user likes the effects of a drug, he or she may move to casual, recreational or regular use.

Casual use is taking a drug only when a person feels like it or when it is offered. Recreational use is drug use for enjoyment in social situations. Regular use means taking drugs almost every day. Habitual or problem drug use occurs when the user becomes dependent (needs to have some of the drug every day).

TIM RATHBONE, BRITISH MP:

"There needs to be an awareness that drugs affect us all, whether as young people, parents...or politicians."

THE USER may have very little control over his or her problem drug use. The effects of this dependence can be serious, and sometimes fatal.

With certain drugs, the user can develop a tolerance, or get used to the drug. He or she has to take very large amounts to feel the same effects. These drugs include alcohol, opiates, LSD, caffeine, amphetamines and tranquillisers.

Psychological dependence can develop with any type of drug. The user believes that he or she will not be able to lead a normal life without taking the drug and becomes very upset if it is not available.

Physical dependence, when the body cannot work without a regular supply of the drug, may happen with long-term use. This is common with depressants (left) and analgesics (see page 12). Withdrawal symptoms, which make the user feel unwell, can happen when a regular user stops taking a drug. When a person has an overdose, he or she takes more of the drug than the body can cope with, becomes very ill and may even die.

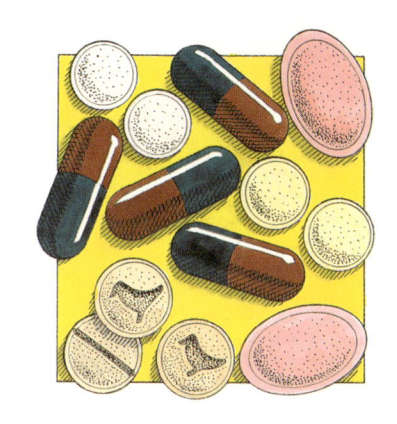

Stimulants excite the nervous system and make users feel awake and energetic for a long time. Caffeine, nicotine (found in tobacco, below) and amyl nitrite (or 'poppers', below) are legal. Illegal stimulants include amphetamines, cocaine, crack (below) and Ecstasy (MDMA or E, top). Anabolic steroids may be used legally, but sporting bodies have banned them.

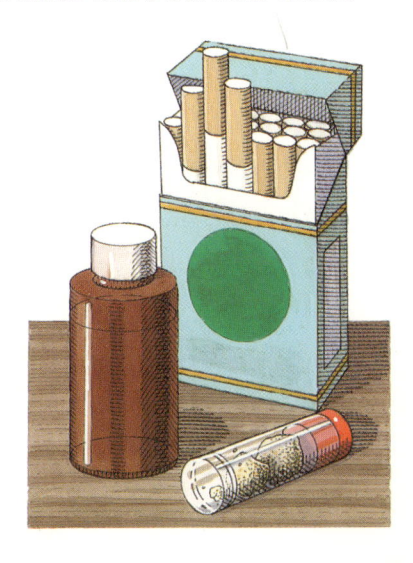

Smoking crack, an illegal, cocaine-based stimulant.

What is a Drug?

The History of Drug Use

Analgesics reduce the user's reactions to pain, discomfort and anxiety. Opium, heroin and codeine (below) are obtained from opium poppies (above). Methadone and pethidine are synthetic (chemical rather than natural) analgesics. Many analgesics have medical uses.

WRITTEN RECORDS and historical research suggest that people all over the world have been using drugs for thousands of years, both as medicines and for leisure purposes. Over the centuries, laws and attitudes about drugs have changed many times.

There is evidence that as long ago as 8000 BC, Amerindians in Central America used mescal beans as a stimulant. Sumerian stone tablets from 4000 BC show that opium was taken for calmness and pain relief. Coca leaves, and the powdered lime used to make them into cocaine, have been found with mummies buried in Peru in 500 BC.

Tobacco has been used by Native North American peoples for hundreds of years. It was introduced into Europe by the European explorer Christopher Columbus, who visited America in 1492. European farmers grew it as a medicine to help people relax; it was not until the 1600s that Europeans began to smoke it. Tobacco laws have changed many times, as medical science has developed. Nicotine is now known to be the drug that kills the most people.

Cocaine was one of the original ingredients of Coca-Cola.

Alcohol also has a long history. Pictures of alcohol production have been found on pieces of pottery made as long ago as 4200 BC in ancient Mesopotamia (the area that is now eastern Syria, southeastern Turkey and most of Iraq).

What is a Drug?

During US prohibition, many people made alcohol at home.

Throughout its history, there have been many attempts to limit people's use of alcohol. In 1920 alcohol was banned in the USA, with a law called 'prohibition'. This led to the illegal smuggling of alcohol from abroad, and the growth of a whole new industry of home-made drinks. Prohibition ended in 1933. In several countries, religion forbids the drinking of alcohol. The laws uphold these beliefs, with strict punishments for people who sell or drink alcohol.

Many drugs that today are illegal were used originally for medical and social purposes. In the nineteenth century, cannabis was often used to relieve pain and cure illnesses. Until 1904, cocaine was a main ingredient of Coca-Cola, which was advertised as a 'pick-me-up'. When LSD (lysergic acid diethylamide) was developed in 1943, it was secretly tested on US soldiers as a possible way to weaken enemy armies.

Tobacco has a long history.

Hallucinogens *affect the way the user sees and hears. They can cause hallucinations (visions), strange dreams or nightmares. The chemical drug LSD (above) can affect users for up to 8 hours.*

'Magic' mushrooms (below) are several kinds of wild mushroom. They have an effect like LSD, but it lasts for a shorter time. **Cannabis**, *or marijuana, is a mild hallucinogen taken from plants. It is often smoked in cigarettes called 'spliffs' (below). It makes the user feel more relaxed and talkative.*

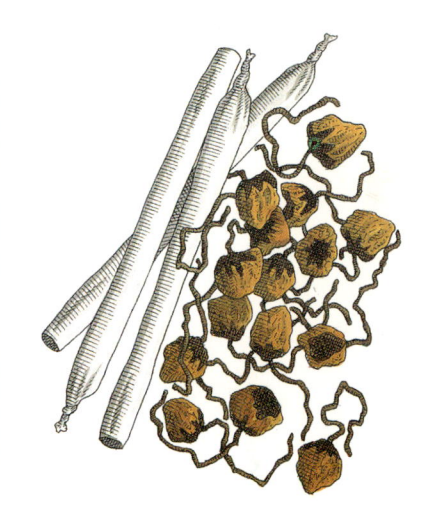

Illness and Death

The Risks to Health

WHILE MOST DRUGS are taken for their positive effects, all drugs carry potential health risks. Short-term and long-term effects, sudden reactions, careless use and impurities may increase the danger.

Countries with more alcohol use tend to have a high rate of alcoholism and liver diseases, which can be fatal. Tobacco is directly linked to breathing difficulties and lung cancer. Yet these problems can be tackled. In Australia, education and new laws have recently reduced the number of deaths associated with alcohol and tobacco.

The number of deaths caused by illegal drug use is increasing all over the world. Other effects on health are difficult to measure, as people will not admit that their illness is due to illegal drug use.

Sniffing solvents puts a great strain on the heart, and could lead to a heart attack. Solvents may also contain poisons. Gases can cause painful swelling of the throat. Long-term cannabis use may cause memory loss and breathing problems. Stimulants can lead to disturbed sleep and intense feelings of anxiety.

The use of Ecstasy can cause the body to overheat. Several young people have died from this heatstroke. Women who take it may have irregular periods. Hallucinogens can cause paranoia (anxiety attacks). Heroin makes people sick and unable to go to the toilet.

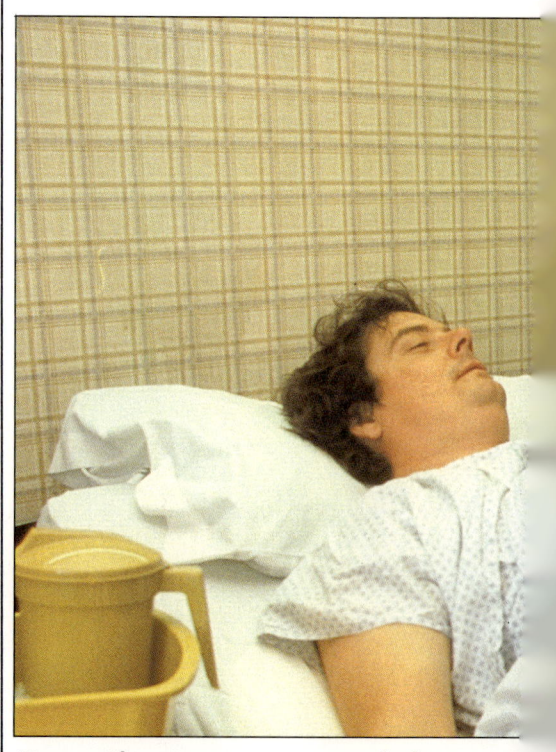

Detoxification centres can help

"I'll tell you...[I] had a lot of fun. I really did. I had a lot of fun, but it's not worth it in the long run, it isn't. You're just screwing yourself over, you go nowhere fast. Usually, you think you're going somewhere, but you don't know where, and you don't care."

Kevin first took marijuana at the age of 13. He later started using other drugs, missed school, and by the age of 14 had been arrested several times for theft. He drank daily, took medical drugs, and used and sold marijuana and cocaine. He began to overdose regularly. At 20, Kevin realised that his drug use was out of control. With the support of his family, he started a treatment programme, which ended his addiction.

Adverse Effects

DRUG USE has many hidden dangers, apart from the obvious risks to health.

While people are under the influence of any drug, their judgment and behaviour may be affected. This leads to a higher risk of accident and injury. This is equally true of alcohol, medicines, solvents and illegal drugs.

Sharing infected needles, for heroin and other drugs, puts users at risk from blood infections like Hepatitis B and HIV.

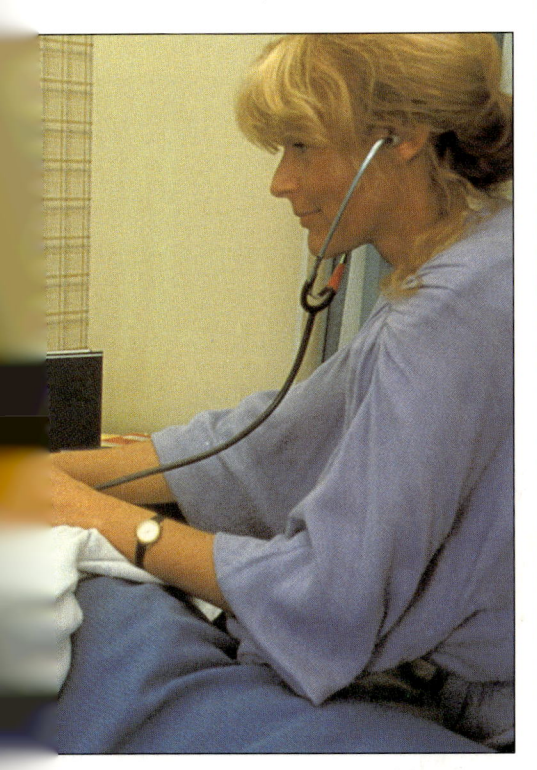

people to beat their addictions.

Sniffing solvents and gases can sometimes be fatal.

Another danger is the effect that a drug can have on a user who already has poor health. Some drugs can reveal hidden health problems, often with fatal effects.

For example, hallucinogens may be very damaging to someone with a mental illness, and they can trigger mental problems in a person whose condition has previously been hidden. People with heart problems, known or unknown, can suffer heart attacks as a result of using powerful stimulants, especially when this is followed by energetic exercise such as dancing. Ecstasy can cause people who suffer from epilepsy to have fits.

People with asthma may also be seriously affected by drugs, especially substances that are smoked or sniffed such as cannabis, nicotine or solvents.

"I realised that my whole family was alcoholic. I didn't much care about any of them except my mother. It really hurt to think of her as a drunk. I started to cry."

Kirk, an adult alcoholic, was a victim of one of the hidden dangers of drug abuse – the distressing effect it can have on the people close to the user.

"What do they usually fight about? About me...My mother thinks it's my father's fault, 'cause I got in trouble, and my father thinks it's her fault. So I get in trouble."

When he was 13, Norris met a group of friends who persuaded him to try various types of drug and to commit crimes such as car theft and vandalism. Norris tried hard to give up this lifestyle, but the pressure from his friends was too strong for him to do so. His drugs and crime habits put a great strain on his parents, and caused many family arguments.

Like Kirk, Norris's story shows one of the hidden problems of drug abuse, for users and their families.

EDDIE ELLISON, 1993:

"If this is a war, a war on drugs, then we are losing...It might be time to consider an alternative."
(Eddie Ellison is a former British Drugs Squad officer.)

Laws and Restrictions

EACH COUNTRY makes its own decisions about which drugs are illegal. These can vary greatly.

Alcohol is legal in most Western countries, but its use is restricted in various ways. Most countries have a minimum age at which a person can buy alcohol. Restrictions also apply to the sale of tobacco in many countries.

Cannabis is generally illegal in Western countries. In the USA, however, the federal autonomy policy means that individual states are free to make their own laws. Some have decided to legalise the use of cannabis.

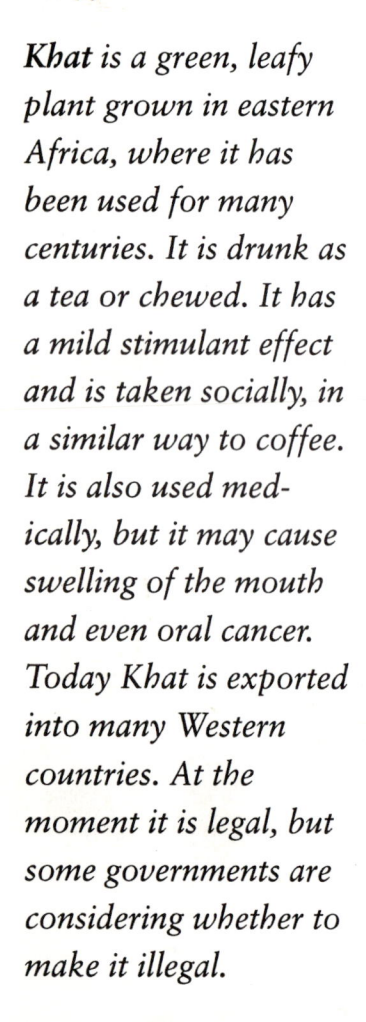

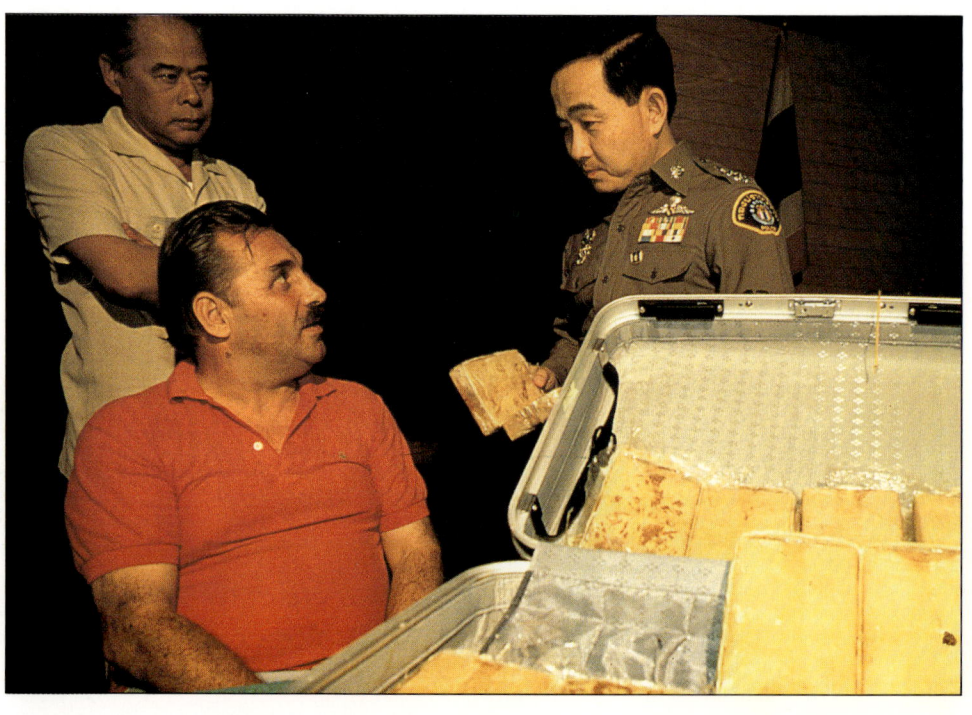

Khat is a green, leafy plant grown in eastern Africa, where it has been used for many centuries. It is drunk as a tea or chewed. It has a mild stimulant effect and is taken socially, in a similar way to coffee. It is also used medically, but it may cause swelling of the mouth and even oral cancer. Today Khat is exported into many Western countries. At the moment it is legal, but some governments are considering whether to make it illegal.

Some countries deal very strictly with people who smuggle drugs.

US ANTI-DRUGS CAMPAIGNER:

"Drug dealers are killing our kids. Is it not the job of the military to protect this country, its future, its kids, for God's sake?"

Tobacco is smoked in hookahs (pipes) in the Middle East.

Religion often influences people's ideas about drugs. Alcohol is forbidden by the Qur'an, the Muslim holy book. This means that it is illegal in many Islamic countries and states, and is banned among Muslim groups in non-Islamic countries. The Mormons, a Christian group, forbid the use of all drugs. Yet the Rastafarian faith approves of cannabis. People of all religions are now spread around the world. For young people, these conflicting beliefs may sometimes seem confusing or irrelevant.

Punishments for drug offences depend on how a country views drug use. In Malaysia and Thailand, for example, public flogging (beating) is a common punishment for minor offences. Smuggling drugs such as heroin can lead to life sentences or execution.

In the Netherlands, drug use is seen as a medical problem rather than a criminal offence, and is treated in a sensitive way. It is illegal to deal in cannabis, Ecstasy and heroin, but government-approved cannabis is available in licensed cafés, to make sure that people who do use it are protected. To separate the cannabis users from the dealers, who might offer users more dangerous drugs like heroin, people in possession of only small amounts of cannabis are not prosecuted. There are special areas at raves where people can check the purity of their Ecstasy. Heroin users can obtain a free regular supply of methadone (see page 21), so that they do not have to use impure heroin or share dirty needles to inject the drug. They are also given free, confidential (secret) medical advice.

In Britain, supplying drugs can lead to imprisonment and large fines. Many people in Britain want cannabis to be made legal, and some police officers agree with this view.

Dramatic methods are used to help drug users in Thailand.

Policing the Traffic

Tracking the Cargoes

Customs officers chasing a drug-smuggling ship. The ships are often very fast, and can be difficult to catch.

MANY COUNTRIES work together to combat the production and distribution of illegal drugs, using sophisticated techniques and equipment.

Some illegal drugs, especially chemical ones like Ecstasy, LSD and amphetamines, are produced in the country where they are used. Many countries have special police to track these drugs. The natural drugs cannabis, cocaine and heroin are grown in a warm climate before being processed. They are then smuggled around the world in a variety of ways. Some are carried in suitcases with false sections, or are swallowed by the carriers. Cars, trucks, boats and planes are fitted with hidden compartments, and packets of drugs are hidden in everyday goods such as tins of food.

The smuggling routes
The opium poppy is grown in Asia. The raw opium is processed into heroin, then is taken via several countries to the customer. Coca leaves are picked in South America, then processed into cocaine. Cannabis (marijuana) is grown in suitable climates.

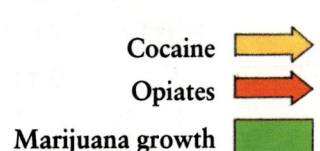

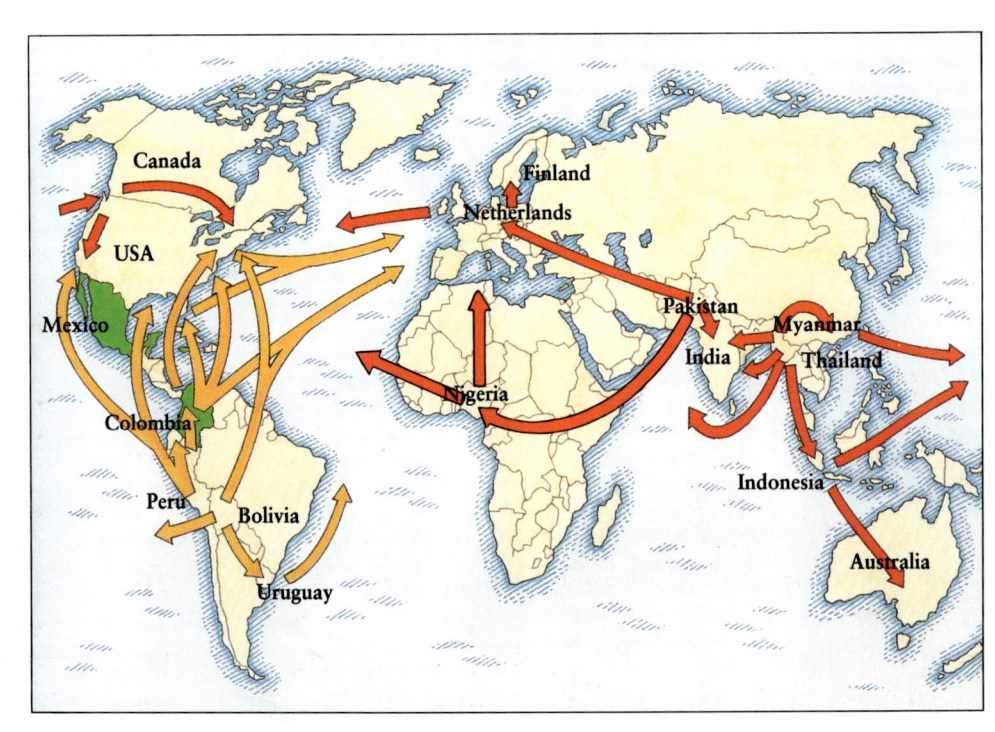

Cocaine ➡
Opiates ➡
Marijuana growth ▇

The major drugs trafficking routes cover most of the world.

Policing the Traffic

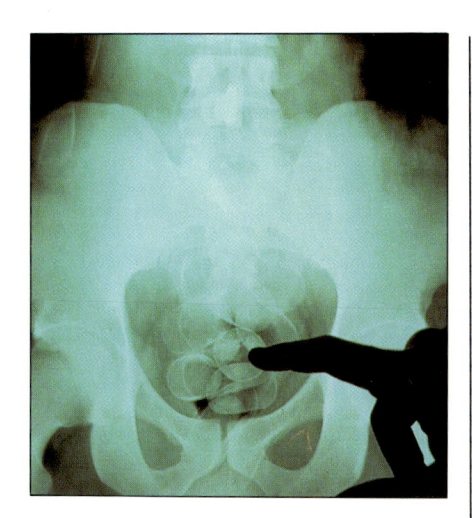

This smuggler has swallowed condoms full of drugs.

Some smugglers wrap their drugs in condoms or plastic bags and then swallow them. Customs departments use X-rays to detect these. It is important that this practice is stopped, as several people have died when the wrappings have burst in their stomachs.

Police and customs departments around the world send each other useful information and share their equipment. With international cooperation, drug smugglers are often tracked secretly across huge distances. However, although there are frequent customs successes, which are well publicised, many more smuggled drugs go undetected.

Planes and boats are used to transport drugs around the world. Small aircraft can land on remote airfields to escape detection. Large ships anchor far from the coastline, and smaller boats transport the cargoes to the shore. Some smugglers may try bribery to persuade officials to 'turn a blind eye' to their activities.

Many customs departments use specially trained sniffer dogs. The animals use their sense of smell to find drugs hidden in luggage, on people and in vehicles. They are taught never to harm anybody. In most cases, their findings are very precise.

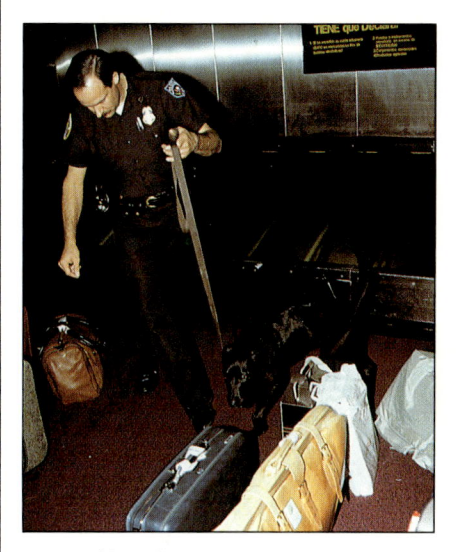

A sniffer dog at work.

Drugs seized in Amsterdam.

All over the world, there is a constant rise in the number of people caught in possession of or selling illegal drugs. As the demand for drugs gets greater, more and more people are prepared to take risks to supply them, and new substances are developed at regular intervals.

People charged with drug offences in Britain, 1988-1992 (latest available statistics)

Drug	1988	1989	1990	1991	1992
Cocaine	591	786	860	838	913
Heroin	1856	1769	1605	1466	1415
LSD	240	435	915	1200	1428
Ecstasy	—	—	286	559	1516
Amphetamines	2538	2395	2330	3532	5653
Cannabis	26111	33669	40194	42209	41353
Methadone	162	172	154	145	191
Other	1266	1307	1452	1296	1242
All drugs	30515	38415	44922	47616	48924

Help and Support

Where to Turn

An adviser (above) takes a call at a crack helpline in New York, USA.

Some governments and charities support drug telephone helplines. These services are free, and often the phone call is free as well. Many lines are staffed for 24 hours a day. Some are for specific groups, such as young people or parents and carers. Some deal with one type of drug use. They are confidential – the adviser will not ask the caller for his or her name. The adviser listens to the caller's worries, and may give him or her advice. But many callers just want to talk to somebody about their situation.

ORGANISATIONS EXIST in most countries to provide information about drugs, to support people affected by drugs, and to help those who want to control or reduce their drug use.

Most people who take drugs for recreation do not see their drug use as a problem. Many of those who are dependent on alcohol or illegal drugs do not wish to stop, or are put off by the thought of treatment. Others seek help to make their drug use safer, or to stop their habit. People who know a drug user may want to help him or her. In a society which disapproves of the use of illegal drugs and the abuse of legal ones, it can be difficult to find the right help.

However, support is available in most countries on both a local and national basis. Government departments distribute public information. Telephone helplines can provide information about drug use and the addresses of local support centres.

Drugs counselling agencies know that they can assist a user only if he or she is willing. They help the users to understand their situation, and to explore ways in which they can change it.

These young people at a Chinese centre have beaten their drugs habits.

Help and Support

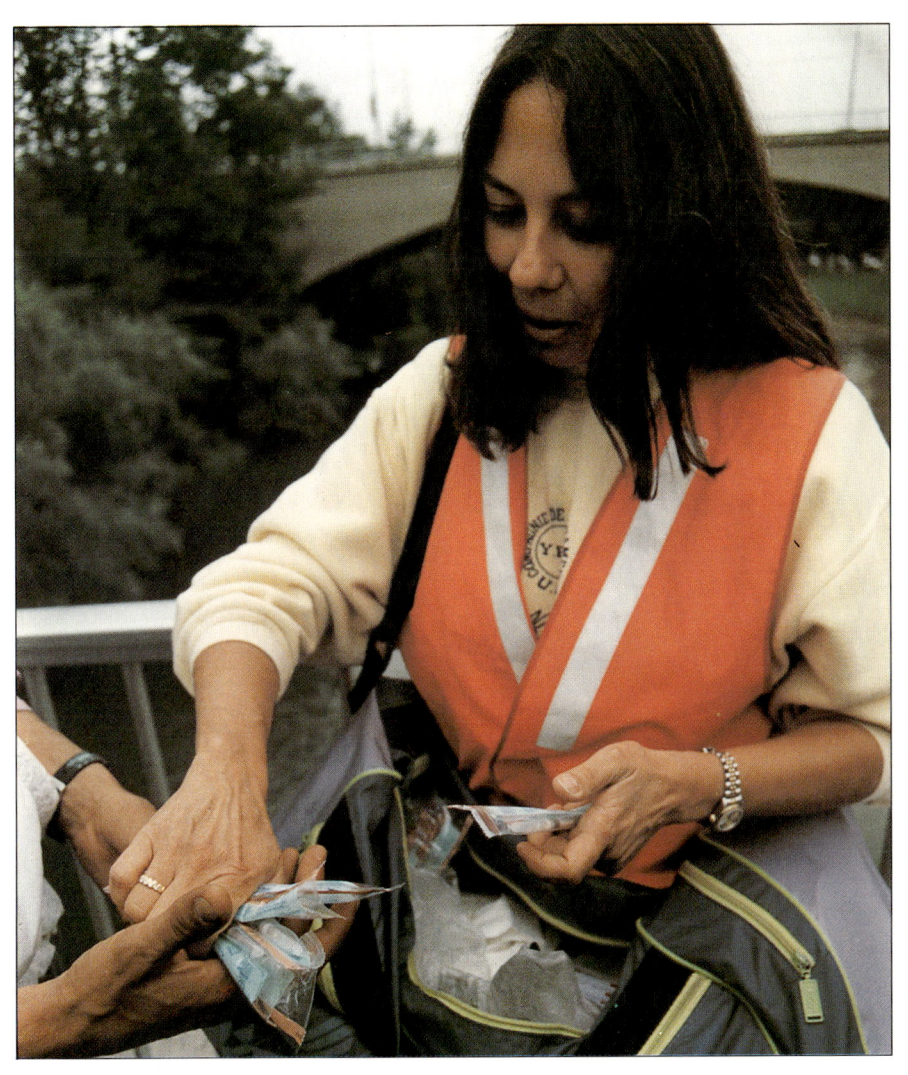

Clean needles are given to heroin users in Zurich, Switzerland, to prevent the spread of Hepatitis B, HIV and other infections.

Methadone (below) is a synthetic analgesic (see page 12). It is prescribed by some doctors as a replacement for heroin, especially in the Netherlands. It means that the user does not have to rely on illegal sources of heroin, which can often involve other dangers. Methadone is drunk as a liquid, avoiding the health risks of injection. Because it is supplied by doctors, users do not put themselves at risk to obtain it, and do not get into debt. A single dose of the drug lasts longer than a similar amount of heroin. However, some users begin to like the effects of methadone and become dependent on it, so its use must be tightly controlled.

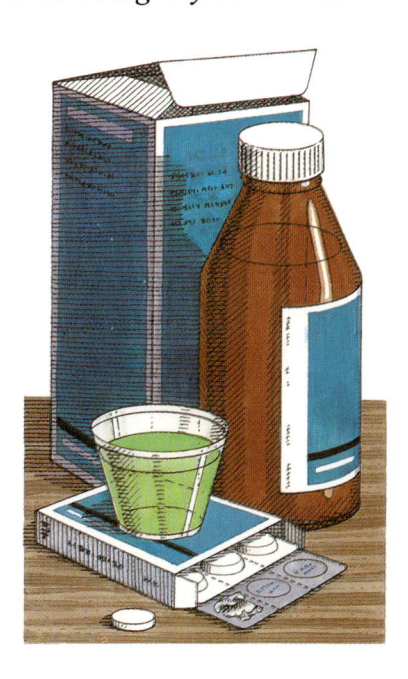

Doctors may sometimes send users to drug clinics, known as rehabilitation centres. These offer various ways of helping people to break their habits, ranging from counselling to medical treatments.

Group therapy is a good way to help users. All the members of the group are in similar situations, and talk together about their problems. It is often hard for drug users to ask people's advice, and so group therapy can be very important.

Organisations have been set up to deal with every form of drug use. They all use different methods, which means that each person is able to choose the type of help that will best suit him or her.

Whatever form of help a user chooses, he or she will need support from family, friends and the local community. It is therefore important to teach people about drug use in a sensitive, balanced way, so that they can offer this support.

Debate and Controversy

Conflicts of Opinion

PEOPLE'S RESPONSES to the drug situation depend on the amount of information they have, their political views, their own experiences of the problem, and current local laws.

There are many rumours and myths about drugs. These are often used to prevent drug abuse. However, it is important that people are correctly informed, so that they can make balanced decisions and offer help and support to those who need it.

IT IS NOT TRUE:
– that crack (above) is instantly addictive;
– that if you try a 'spliff' (a cannabis cigarette) you will certainly move on to heroin addiction and die as a result of it.

It is safer to avoid taking illegal drugs, but it is important to know the facts.

There are various theories about the best way to tackle drug abuse and to help users.

In current medical opinion, drug misuse is a 'disease' which needs 'treatment' with medicines and clinics. In contrast, pathological methods suggest that users have 'addictive personalities', or they have no control over their actions. They help them to realise this and so to tackle their addictions.

The criminal treatment of drug use blames and punishes the user for breaking the law.

There is much debate about which of these methods is best. Some people see drugs as pleasant and harmless, and disagree with those who take the criminal view. Politicians may change their views according to what they think voters want to hear, which can be very confusing.

In 1994 the mayor of Maastricht, in Belgium, declared 'war' on drugs.

Debate and Controversy

A demonstration for the legalisation of cannabis in the USA. The cannabis issue has caused worldwide debate.

The Alternatives

WHAT IS THE best alternative to the 'war' on drugs? Is it drugs education for all; information and help for drug users; stricter laws and punishments; or keeping the situation as it is now?

Many people argue that if all drugs were legalised, there would be no criminal activity and those involved would not be in danger from illness or violence. Governments would introduce standard quality controls and taxes, like those on alcohol and tobacco. Problem users would be treated by health services. Drugs education could be accurate and balanced, to allow young people to develop their own opinions.

However, politicians, religious leaders and the majority of the general public would find this freedom very difficult to accept, after years of influence from the media. Others argue that it would encourage drug abuse among young people.

It seems that the world might never agree about the best way to deal with the drugs situation, but it is important that it is debated with sensitivity and intelligence.

Information and advice about drugs may be obtained from health services, teachers, drug agencies and helplines.

ISDD
*(Institute for the Study of Drug Dependence)
Waterbridge House
32–36 Loman Street
London SE1 0EE
Tel. 0171 928 1211*

Health Education Authority
*Hamilton House
Mabledon Place
London WC1H 9TX
Tel. 0171 383 3833*

*Scottish Health Education Group
Health Education Centre
Woodburn House
Canaan Lane
Edinburgh EH10 4SG
Tel. 0131 447 8044*

*Australia
All the states, and some of the major cities, have their own Alcohol and Drug Information Service, which will be listed in the telephone book.*

TOPICS... HOT TOPICS... HOT TOPICS... HOT

In the News: Drugs in the Public Eye 24

Sports Stars Join the Campaign

The athlete Carl Lewis.

Sporting champions and personalities, such as the US athlete Carl Lewis (above), are now campaigning for their sports to be 'cleaned up' from the misuse of drugs. They want to be seen as positive role models for young people and to encourage fair play in the sporting world. International sporting organisations have banned many substances, and random drugs testing can occur at any time. The winners of competitions are tested automatically, and if any traces of proscribed (banned) drugs are found in their body, they can face long-term suspension from their sport. Some banned substances are used in the making of legal medicines, so sportsmen and women must always be careful when taking medication of any kind before a competition.

Sporting Glory Spoilt by Drug Misuse

SEVERAL RECENT cases have suggested that the use of illegal drugs is increasing among sportsmen and women. In their search for glory for themselves, their team and their country, some people will do anything to win – including breaking the rules.

In 1994, several Chinese athletes were suspected of using performance-improving drugs in international competitions, although this was never proved. A member of the British women's athletics team was accused of taking banned substances in the same year. Such cases mean that sudden improvements in performance are now treated as suspicious.

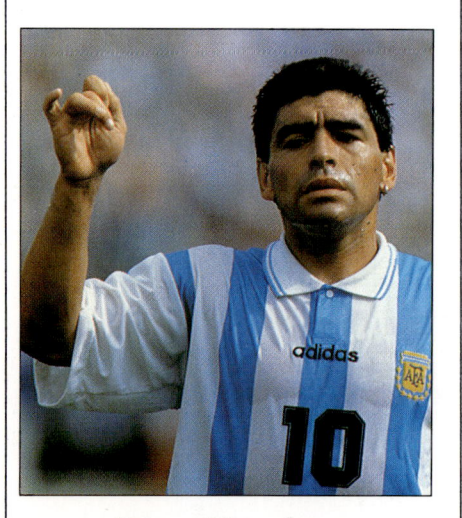

The Chinese athletics team.

Diego Maradona.

The great Argentinian footballer Diego Maradona was banned from the 1994 World Cup for using cocaine. Many people feel that the wealth now offered to sportsmen and women through sponsorship can lead them to take banned drugs. They may be scared of losing their reputation, and so take drugs to maintain their performance in public.

TOPICS... HOT TOPICS... HOT TOPICS... HOT

In the News: Drugs in the Public Eye

River Phoenix, whose death shocked Hollywood.

Film Star Dies at 23

IN 1994, the film actor River Phoenix was killed by a lethal cocktail of illegal drugs. Was this a result of a highly pressurised life in the public eye?

Phoenix had always denied ever using drugs. His death, and the deaths of other actors and musicians, suggests that the entertainment industry and its pressures to 'be the best' can lead people into drug dependence. The private lives of entertainers are reported on continuously, while the need to perform well at all times may often cause them to use stimulants to help them stay alert, then other drugs to help them relax. Many people worry that the use of drugs by film stars sets a bad example to young people, who may see drug abuse as glamorous without considering its long-term effects. The death of River Phoenix might change all that.

A Pattern of Misuse

Kurt Cobain

Kurt Cobain, lead singer of the US rock group Nirvana, used heroin to relieve stomach pains. He described one of his experiences of drug abuse: "You just lay in bed and drool all over yourself." Cobain committed suicide in 1994.

Rock guitarist Jimi Hendrix died of a drug overdose at the height of his fame in 1970.

Jimi Hendrix.

TOPICS... HOT TOPICS... HOT TOPICS... HOT

Latest News: A Growing Occurrence?

An Increase in Crime

Worldwide, illegal drugs are as readily available as legal ones, and can often be cheaper and easier for young people to obtain. Customs seizures are increasing, but these represent only a small percentage of the total amount of illegal drugs transported around the world. Police are catching and jailing more users and suppliers every year. The number of known addicts is increasing, as are the deaths caused by illegal drugs. Are these drugs now becoming as 'normal' a part of modern life as alcohol and tobacco?

Are Drugs and Crime Related?

It is often suggested that the links between drugs and crime are simple. People need money to buy drugs, and turn to crime to get it. This criminal activity is seen as a direct result of the drug use. On the other hand, perhaps people who already break the law regularly find it easier to start taking illegal drugs than people who do not. It is hard to know which theory is correct.

Drug abuse, and the dangers it involves, is increasing constantly.

New Data Reveals Dramatic Changes in Drug Use

DRUG HELPLINES and organisations are busier than ever, due to the rapidly changing drugs scene and the increase in drug use and its related dangers.

Drug agencies were set up originally to deal with dependence on analgesics such as heroin and depressants like alcohol. Some helped users to limit or reduce their use, while others only helped those who were drug free. Most clients were adults wanting to change their dependent lifestyle.

Recent studies have shown that drug users are now likely to be younger and to use cannabis, stimulants and hallucinogens. They often do not see their drug use as a problem, may not want to give up their drugs, and often want information to help them use drugs as safely as possible.

TOPICS... HOT TOPICS... HOT TOPICS... HOT

Latest News: A Growing Occurrence?

Addiction is Not the Only Source of Danger

Isolated or dirty places like this can be very dangerous.

THE EFFECTS of drug use on the body are well known, but it also has hidden risks.

People's involvement with drugs can lead them into risky situations. They might buy and sell their drugs in isolated places, or try new substances which can make them ill. There is therefore an urgent need for accurate information and education about drugs, and for more organisations and advice agencies to which users can turn for support.

Drug Users are Defying the Law

For some people, taking illegal drugs for leisure purposes may be the only criminal activity that they are involved with. They see this activity as a very different crime to theft or violence. But if they are caught they will be treated the same as other criminals, and their futures will be affected. Many are prepared to take the risk.

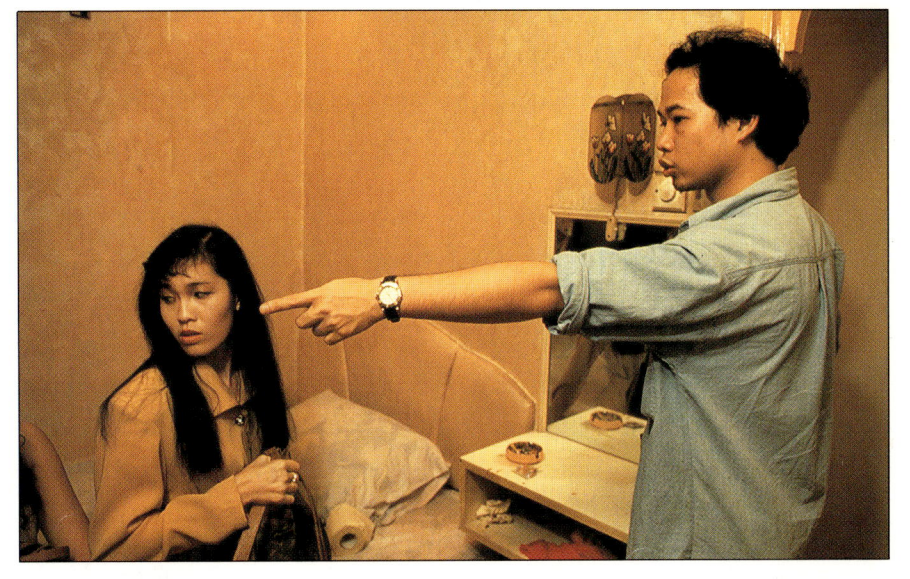

A police officer makes an arrest for drug offences in Hong Kong.

TOPICS... HOT TOPICS... HOT TOPICS... HOT

Latest News: A New Approach

The burning of marijuana plantations has destroyed the homes of many South American workers.

Has the Time Come for a Rethink?

DRUG USE seems to be increasing, despite attempts to restrict it all over the world. Is it time to change our approach to the issue?

Despite the efforts of governments and other organisations to reduce drug use and sale, drug-taking continues to increase. Police, customs, strict laws and attempts to scare people about drug abuse have all failed to make an impact. It may be time to recognise that drugs have been around for many centuries and will not go away. Most people take drugs of some kind. Perhaps we should increase our efforts to educate journalists, politicians, teachers, doctors, parents and carers and young people so that they understand the subject better and can face drugs issues sensibly.

Many people argue that drug laws are unfair. In the 'war' on drugs, there has been much destruction of the homes and crops of the farmers who grow marijuana, coca and opium poppies, while those who produce hops (for beer), grapes (for wine) and tobacco are left alone. Users who are jailed for taking drugs often need advice and support, rather than punishments, to help them face any problems.

TOPICS... HOT TOPICS... HOT TOPICS... HOT

Latest News: A New Approach

Clubs Adopt a Sensitive Approach

MANY VENUES around the world, from rave clubs to youth clubs, are changing their attitudes to drug use as more young people try drugs.

Some rave club owners now realise that many club-goers will take drugs before or during the evening, and have developed new methods of tackling this problem, such as providing teams of safety advisers. Dancers who have taken Ecstasy can get very hot and dehydrated (short of water), and may even die. The advisers are on hand to make sure that they get rest, water and advice.

Youth clubs provide opportunities for young people to talk with others about their views, feelings and worries, and youth workers will often lead discussions about the local drug scene. As long as drugs continue to be available, youth workers help to prevent health problems and other dangers by providing information and advice, and by being friendly and supportive both to users and non-users.

The Amsterdam drugs squad.

Police take a New Attitude

Nowadays, many police forces are choosing to help rather than punish those who use drugs rarely. They may check for drugs among people queuing for clubs. If club-goers overdose or become ill on drugs such as Ecstasy, many forces prefer to help them. They might take the users to the police station, where they offer them water and advice about sensible drug use. This is partly due to the fact that several young people have died recently from the effects of Ecstasy. More and more police officers are working together with teachers to provide balanced, reliable information about drugs for young people in schools.

This US anti-crack poster is designed to appeal to young people.

TOPICS... HOT TOPICS... HOT TOPICS... HOT

Latest News: What Can We Do? 30

An Issue for Everyone

IT IS IMPORTANT to remember that all drugs carry health risks, even when the drugs are medicines. Everybody should know these risks, to be able to avoid them and to help others in danger.

It is essential to find reliable sources of accurate, up-to-date drugs information. Talk to your parents or carers, to hear their views and to let them know yours. Talk to teachers about what your school can provide, and find out what is on offer at your local youth club. Practise being assertive (letting other people know what you think), without unpleasantness.

Try to learn as much as you can about drugs and drug use, and think carefully about the possible results whenever you make important decisions. Choose friends you can rely on when you need help, and be prepared to offer them your support. Try not to follow pressure from others – life can be much more worthwhile and enjoyable when you plan what you want to do.

Remember that people's attitudes to drugs can vary from country to country.

Drugs education classes are now common in many schools.

A Balanced View

When discussing the issue of drugs, it is very important to think about the differing views of people all over the world. While Western countries may condemn the use of certain drugs, others may see them as harmless or as an important source of money. Some religions may impose restrictions that seem unnecessary or harsh to other people. Whatever point of view you take, it is vital to understand the drugs issue on a worldwide scale. Only then will all the countries be able to work together to deal with drugs, reduce their dangers and health risks and help those people involved.

TOPICS... HOT TOPICS... HOT TOPICS... HOT

Latest News and Glossary 31

Alternative 'Highs'

It can be tough to find a way to be 'successful'. Even sports may be satisfying only to the few people who reach the top. But although anyone can take drugs, it is important not to see them as a way of making friends or winning respect. Drugs can never give us a reason for living or a feeling of achievement. Apart from its dangers, drug-taking is not satisfying. Its 'highs' are very short-term, and in the end they have no positive results. Look for other activities that have a controlled risk, give you a sense of excitement and are satisfying to you.

A pro-cannabis demonstrator.

GLOSSARY

Abuse To use something in an excessive or harmful way.
Addiction A habit that is very difficult to break.

Coca The shrub from which cocaine is obtained.
Counselling Helping people to understand their problems by talking about them.

Dependent Unable to live a normal life without a certain substance, object or person.
Detoxification Ridding the body of a poison or drug.

Federal autonomy The US system in which each state is free to make its own laws.

Hallucinations Seeing the world in a different way, or seeing visions.

Illegal Unlawful.
Impurity Something that is mixed into a purer substance.

Legal status The position of something before the law.

Media Newspapers, books, TV, films, magazines etc.
Mescal A type of cactus found in Central America.

Misuse Using something for an unintended purpose.

Opiates Any drugs which come from the opium poppy.

Paranoia Thinking that everybody is 'out to get you'.
Pathological Concerned with medical problems.
'Pick-me-up' A substance which makes the user feel more awake or energetic.
Possession The crime of owning illegal drugs.

Smuggle To transport something illegally into a country.
Sponsorship Paying a person for a task, often to advertise a product.
Supplying Giving or selling drugs to another person, which can be a serious offence.
Synthetic Made by combining chemicals, rather than from natural substances.

Tranquillisers Drugs used to reduce worry or help sleep.

Withdrawal symptoms The effects felt by a user when he or she goes without the drug for a while.

TOPICS... HOT TOPICS... HOT TOPICS... HOT

Index

addiction 10, 14, 27, 31
advertising 8-9
alcohol 2, 5, 6, 8, 10, 11, 12-13, 14, 15, 16, 20
amphetamines 5, 7, 11, 18, 19
amyl nitrite 11
anabolic steroids 2, 11
analgesics 11, 12, 21, 26

barbiturates 10

caffeine 2, 6, 11, 16
cannabis 1, 2, 5, 7, 13, 14, 15, 16, 17, 18, 19, 22, 31
cocaine 2, 11, 12, 18, 19
codeine 12
crack 2, 11, 20, 22, 29
crime 26

dealers 3, 6-7, 17
depressants 10, 11, 26
detoxification centres 14-15
drug misuse 31
  age 4
  controversy 22-3
  counselling 3, 31
  education 3, 20, 23, 27, 28, 30
  effects 10-11, 14-15, 27, 30
  entertainment industry 25
  history 12-13
  punishment 3, 17, 22, 27-8
  reasons 4, 24-5, 31
  restrictions 16-17, 30

solutions 3, 20-21, 23, 28-9, 30
sport 24
drugs
  definition 10
  distribution networks 6
  home-grown 7
  medicines 2, 5, 6, 9, 12, 13, 15, 30

Ecstasy 2, 5, 11, 14, 15, 17, 18, 29
experimentation 10

glue sniffing 2, 10

hallucinogens 13, 14, 15, 26, 31
health risks 14-15, 16, 30
helplines 20, 26
heroin 5, 12, 14, 15, 17, 18, 19, 21, 22, 26
HIV 15, 21

increase in drug use 4-5, 19, 27

legalisation 2, 17, 23, 27, 31
legislation 3, 16-17, 23
levels of drug use 10
LSD 2, 5, 11, 13, 18, 19

'magic' mushrooms 13
marijuana 1, 2, 5, 7, 13, 14, 15, 16, 17, 18, 22, 31
methadone 12, 19, 21

nicotine 2, 3, 5, 6, 8, 13, 14, 15, 16, 17

opiates 11, 12, 18, 31
overdose 11, 14, 25, 29

pethidine 12
physical dependence 11
police 18-19, 29
'poppers' 11

quality of drugs 5, 6

rehabilitation centres 21

smuggling 3, 6, 16-17, 18-19, 26, 31
sniffer dogs 19
solvent sniffing 4, 10, 14, 15
stimulants 11, 12, 14, 15, 16, 26

tobacco 2, 3, 5, 6, 8, 13, 14, 15, 16, 17
tolerance 11
trafficking 3, 6, 16-17, 18-19, 26, 31
tranquillisers 10, 11, 31

withdrawal symptoms 10, 11, 31

Photocredits
Abbreviations: t-top, m-middle, b-bottom, r-right, l-left
All the pictures in this book were supplied by Frank Spooner Pictures, apart from the following pages: 4l, 8br: Roger Vlitos; 8t: Solution Pictures; 8bl, 9, 11b, 16t, 17b, 20t, 23b, 29b: David Browne/Parachute; 12, 13t: Range Pictures; 13b: Mary Evans Picture Library; 25tr, 25b: Rex Features.

Herald
INTERNATIONAL Tribune

PUBLISHED WITH THE NEW YORK TIMES AND THE WASHINGTON POST

London, Thursday, April 13, 1995

'Cleansers' of Muslims Show No Sign of Yielding

By Roger Cohen
New York Times Service

ZVORNIK, Bosnia-Herzegovina — Up through a ghostly terrain of smashed and ransacked former Muslim homes, Branko Grujic led the way, intent on showing off his crowning contribution to what he calls the victory of Serbian Orthodox Christianity over Islam in Bosnia.

Mr. Grujic, the mayor of this northeastern Bosnian town now controlled by Serbs and completely "cleansed" of its 40,000 prewar Muslim inhabitants, has a pet project. It stands atop the escarpment that overlooks Zvornik and the meandering sweep of the Drina River.

Arriving at the summit of the cliff, Mr. Grujic paused to kiss a wooden cross he has had erected before declaring: "The Turks destroyed the Serbian church that was here when they arrived in Zvornik in 1463. Now we are rebuilding the church and reclaiming this as Serbian land forever and

There is indeed a cruel finality to

of thousands of Muslims have been pushed out by force, many of them to Bosnian government-controlled territory around Srebrenica and Tuzla.

Such activity, and the uncompromising attitude of Mr. Grujic, suggest that Serbian readiness to accept new peace proposals from the United States may be scant.

Serbs in general remain committed to holding onto land they have seized by force and

The UN deploys troops around T
in preparation for an aid

appear to have
Bosnian politi
with Mu
"Look
poin
shif

le gouvernement israélien divisé face aux colons extrémistes

Les tractations continuent en Israël à propos de l'entrée au gouvernement du parti Tsomet du général Rafaël

opposé les membres du gouvernement mesures à prendre contre les veille, entre 25 000 et 30 dont quelques milliers à Tel-Aviv pour réc diate des extrémi